Letterland™

My name is

....

Review Level 1   a-z, ck, ng

Review Level 2   ch, sh, th, wh, ph   a_e, ai, ay

e_e, ee, ea, y   i_e, ie, igh, y   o_e, oa, ow   u_e, ue, oo, ew

ar, or, er, ir, ur, wr   o, oo, u, oy, oi   aw, au, ow, ou

Let's learn about...

air ear   ce ci cy

Level 3 - Workbook 1

Let's write these letter shapes.

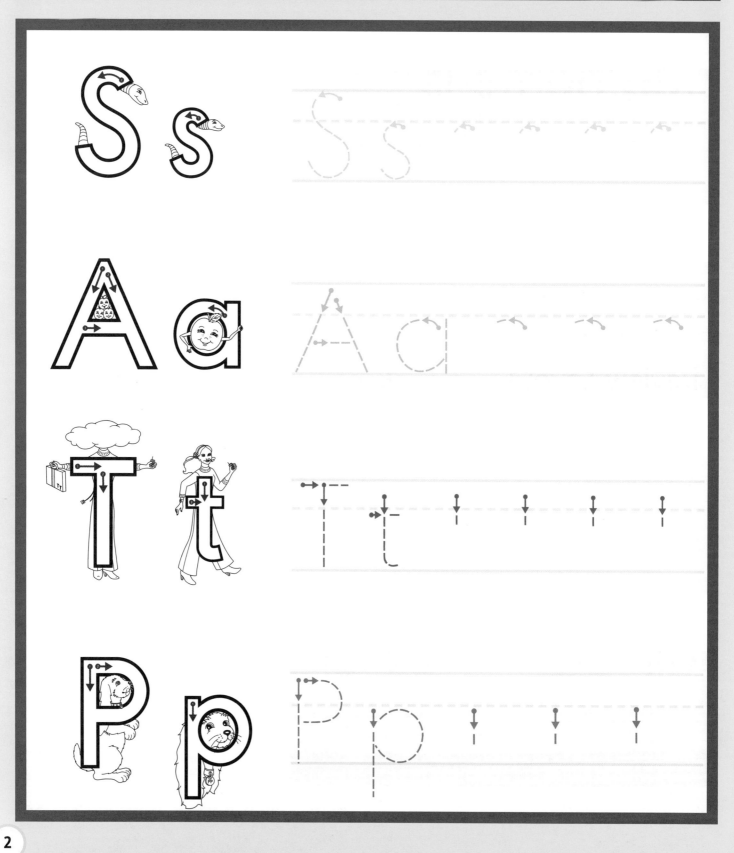

Write **s**, **a**, **t** or **p** on the lines to complete the words.

_ nt

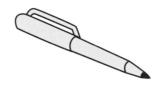
_ en

_ un

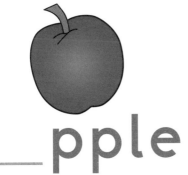
_ pple

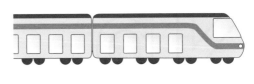
_ rain

_ ree

_ and

_ aint

Let's write these letter shapes.

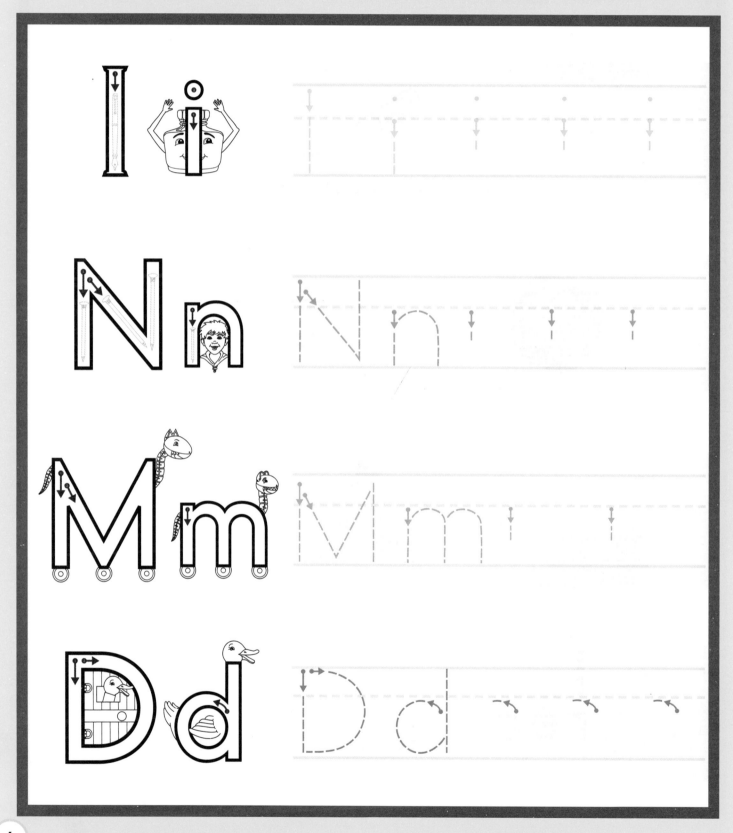

Write **i**, **n**, **m** or **d** on the lines to complete the words.

_ail

_ap

_nk

_nsect

_og

_rum

_ine

_ilk

Let's write these letter shapes.

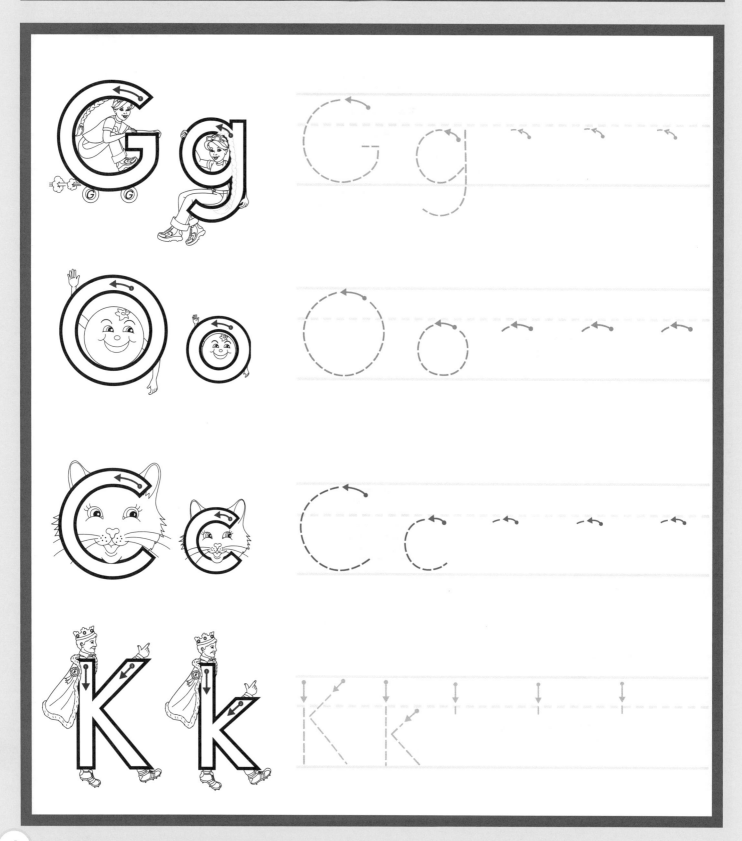

Write **g**, **o**, **c** or **k** on the lines to complete the words.

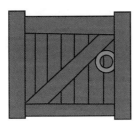

_ ate

_ up

_ n

_ range

_ ettle

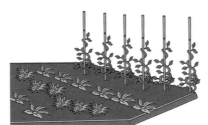

_ arden

_ ar

_ ey

Let's write these letter shapes.

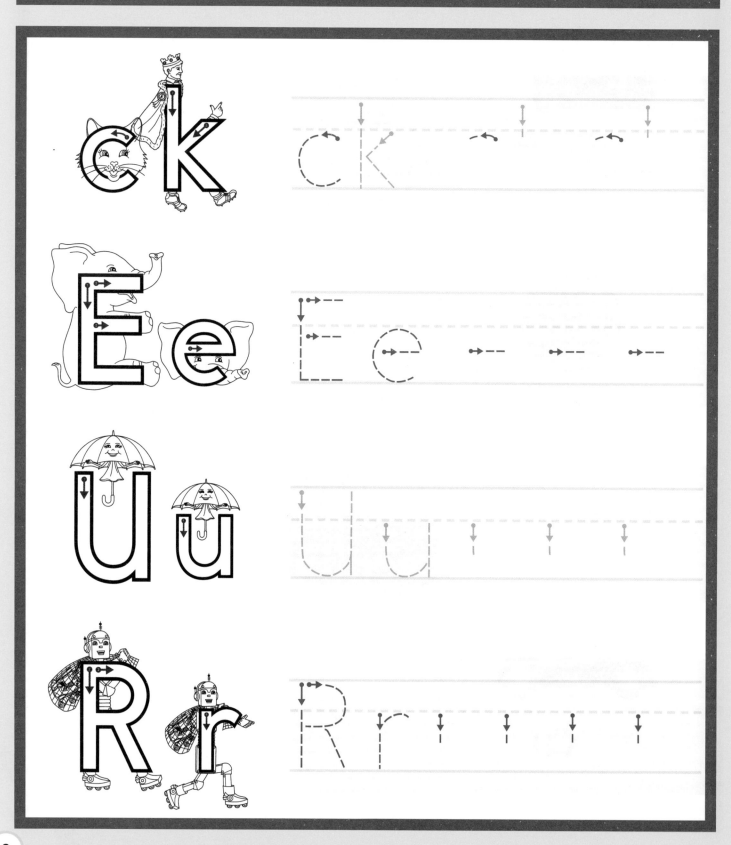

Write **ck**, **e**, **u** or **r** on the lines to complete the words.

_gg

_ice

clo___

_ain

_nder

_mbrella

_lbow

so___

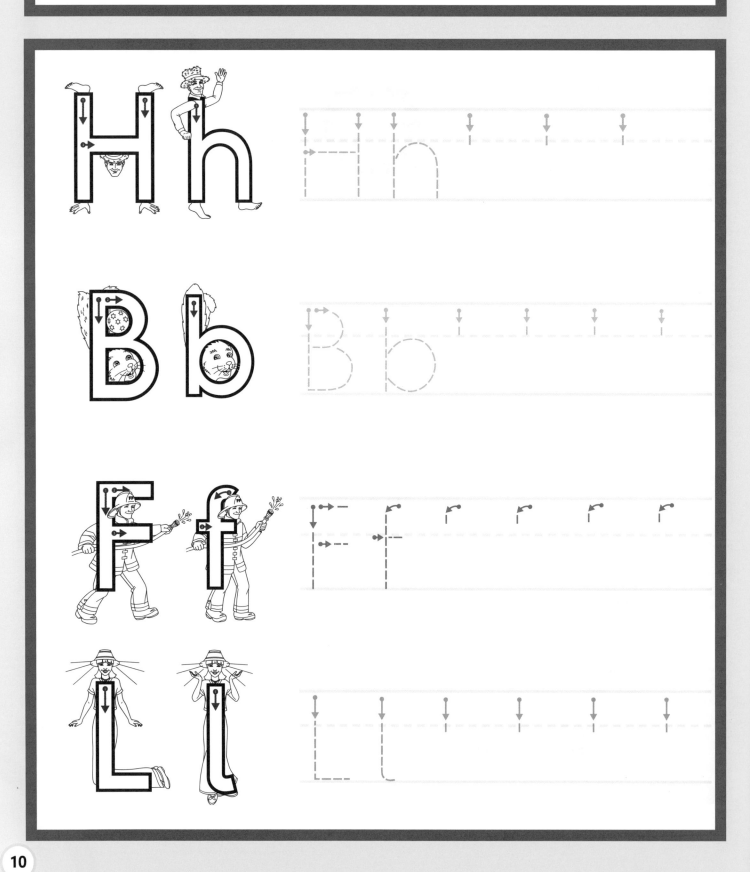

Write **h**, **b**, **f** or **l** on the lines to complete the words.

__og

__ook

__at

__rog

__all

__orse

5

__ive

__eaf

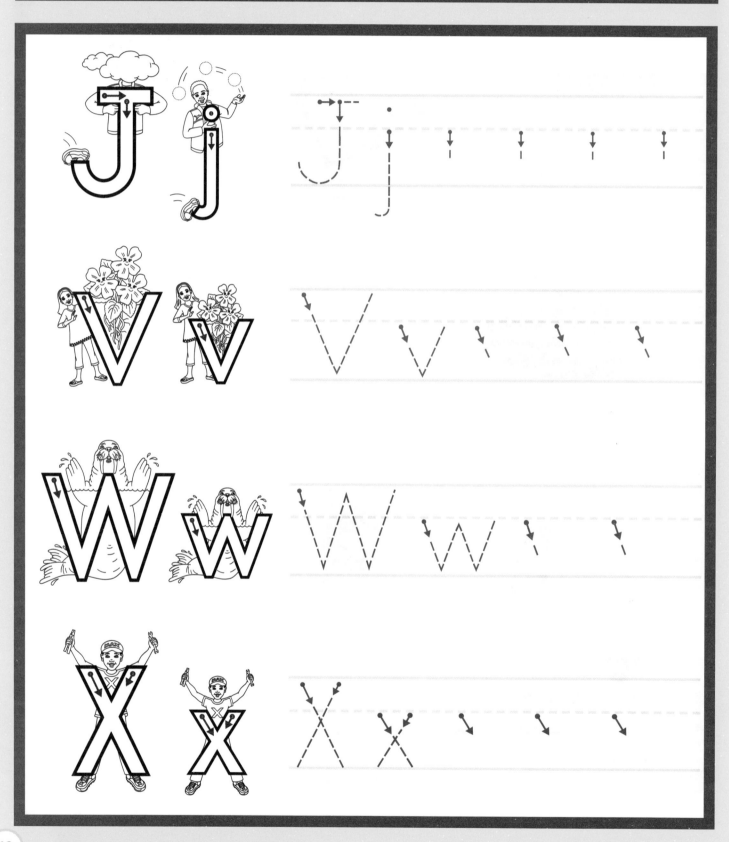

Write **j**, **v**, **w** or **x** on the lines to complete the words.

6

si __

__uice

__an

__iolin

__atch

__am

__indow

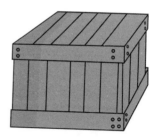

bo__

Let's write these letter shapes.

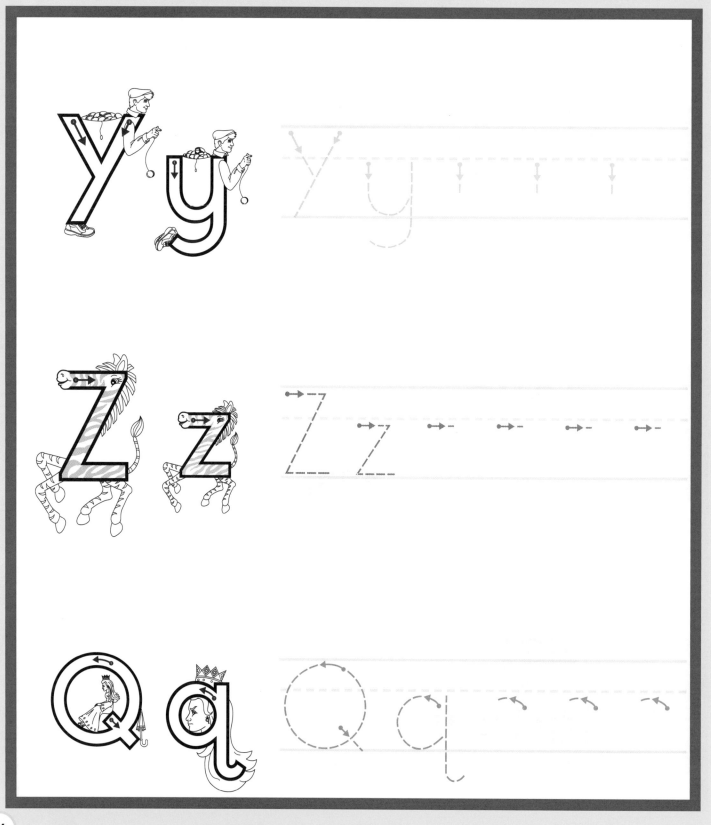

Write **y**, **z**, or **q** on the lines to complete the words.

0
_ero

_oo

_uilt

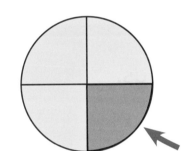
_uarter

_ellow

? _uestion

_o-yo

_ip

Let's write these letter shapes.

 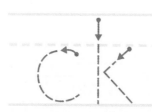

c k

Write **ck** on the lines to complete the words.

so ___

bla ___

lo ___

si ___

16

Let's write these letter shapes.

ng

Write **ng** on the lines to complete the words.

si __ __

ki __ __

ri __ __

wi __ __

Let's write these letter shapes.

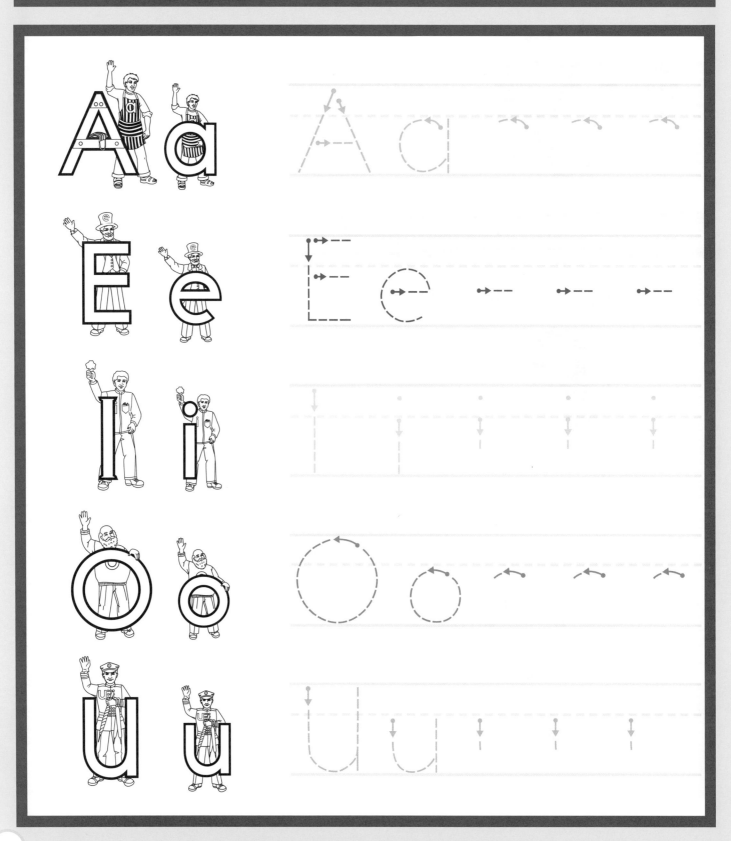

Write **a**, **e**, **i**, **o** or **u** on the lines to complete the words.

__pron

__pen

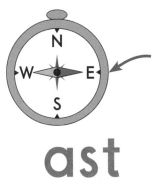

__ast

__sland

__nicycle

__ce cream

__ld

__at

You can write lots of words now! Write the correct letters on the lines to make the words.

You can write lots of words now! Write the correct letters on the lines to make the words.

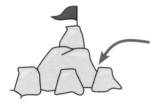

_____

_____

_____

_____

_____

_____

Write the whole alphabet, from Annie Apple to Zig Zag Zebra, on the lines below.

How many words can you make that end in **at**?
Add each of the sounds below to make a new word.

_at

b c h m r s

Fill in the missing words to complete the sentences. The words you need are in the yellow space.

A _____ is _____ a _____ .

A _____ is _____ a _____ .

A _____ is _____ a _____ .

box bed cat dog fox in log on on

Draw a picture to match this sentence.

A hat on a cat!

23

Let's write these letter shapes.

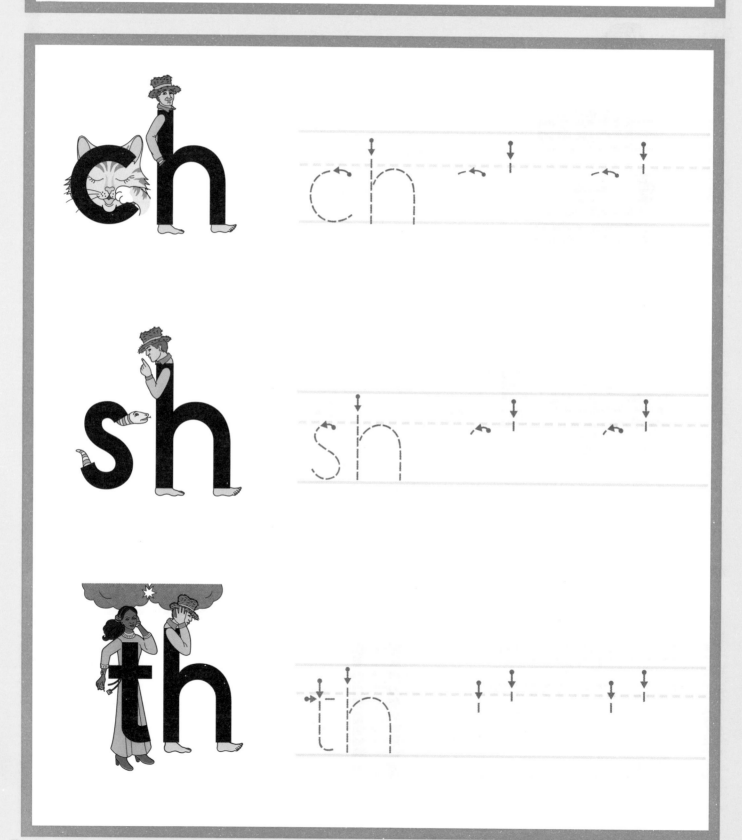

Write **ch**, **sh** or **th** on the lines to complete the words.

___ ___ ell

___ ___ eese

ba ___ ___

___ ___ icken

___ ___ ip

___ ___ under

___ ___ oe

___ ___ op

Let's write these letter shapes.

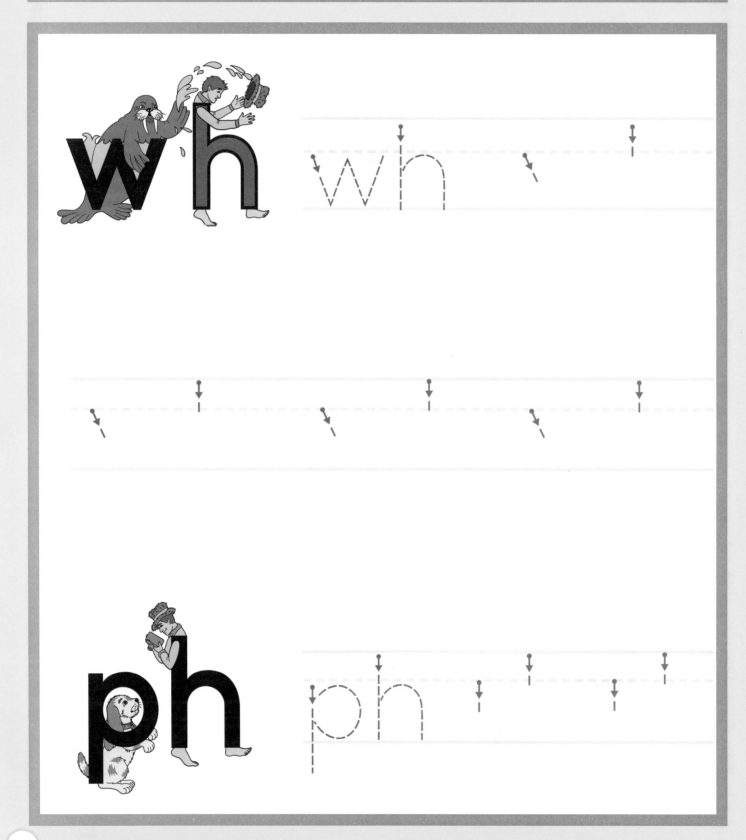

Write **wh** or **ph** on the lines to complete the words.

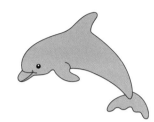

dol___in

___ale

ele___ant

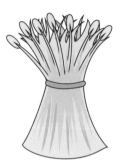

___eat

___oto

___one

___eel

Let's write these letter shapes.

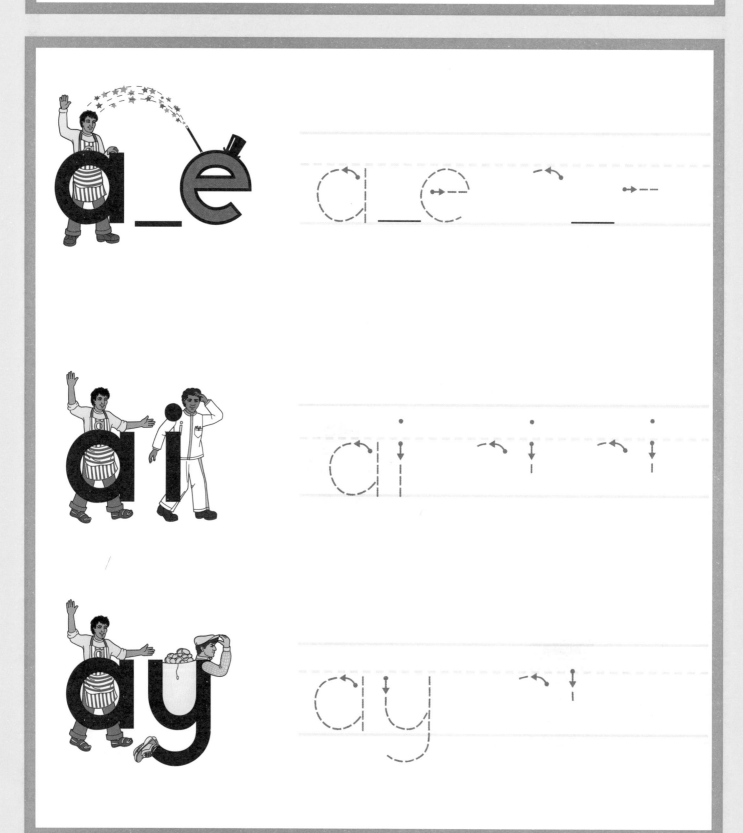

Write **a_e**, **ai** or **ay** on the lines to complete the words.

c_k_

p___nt

spr___

l_k_

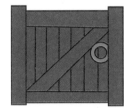

g_t_

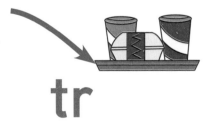

tr___

n___l

Let's write these letter shapes.

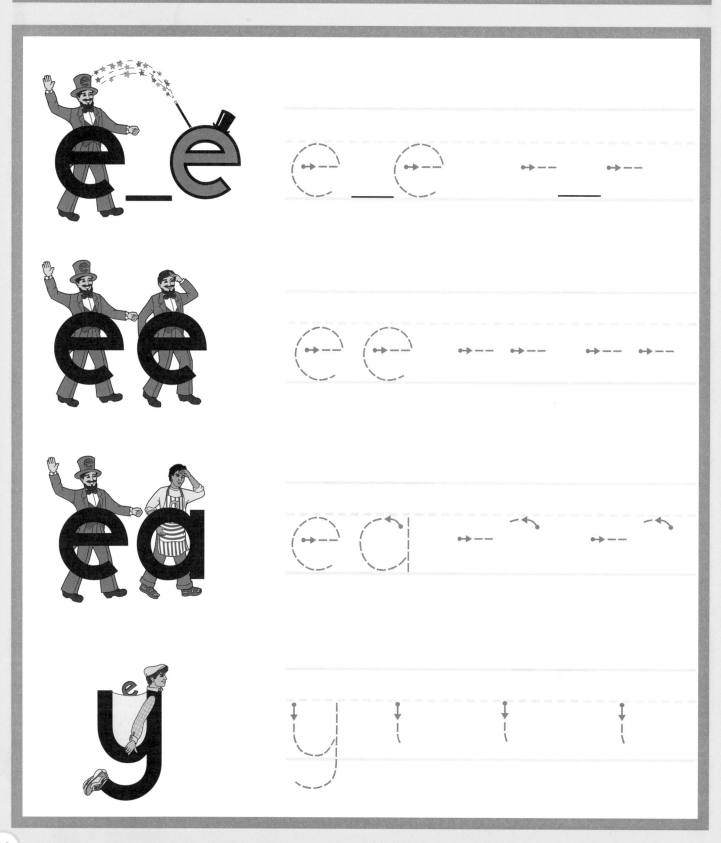

Write **e_e**, **ee**, **ea** or **y** on the lines to complete the words.

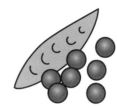

p___s

del_t_

part_

l__f

athl_t_

tedd_

j__p

tr__s

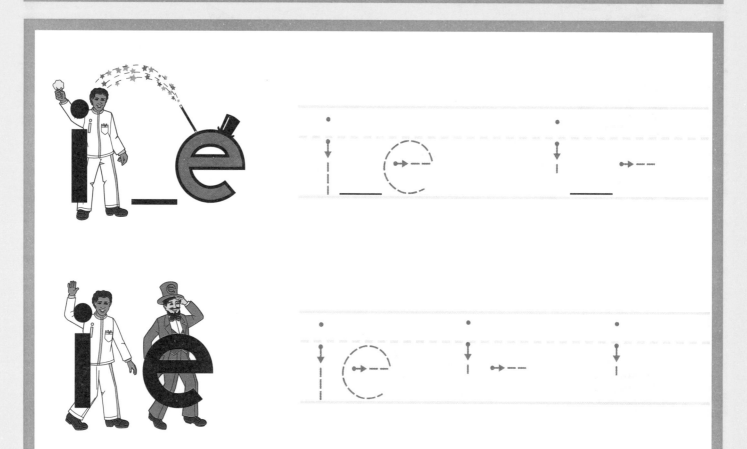

Mr I and Mr E Rule Breaker!

Write **i_e** or **ie** on the lines to complete the words.

sl__d__

t___

k__t__

p___

b__k__

! When Mr I and Mr E go out walking, Mr I usually does the talking. But sometimes Mr E talks in words like:

f____ld

Ann_____

Let's write these letter shapes.

Write **igh** or **y** on the lines to complete the words.

cr__

l____t

fl__

n____t

sk__

f____t

r____t

Let's write these letter shapes.

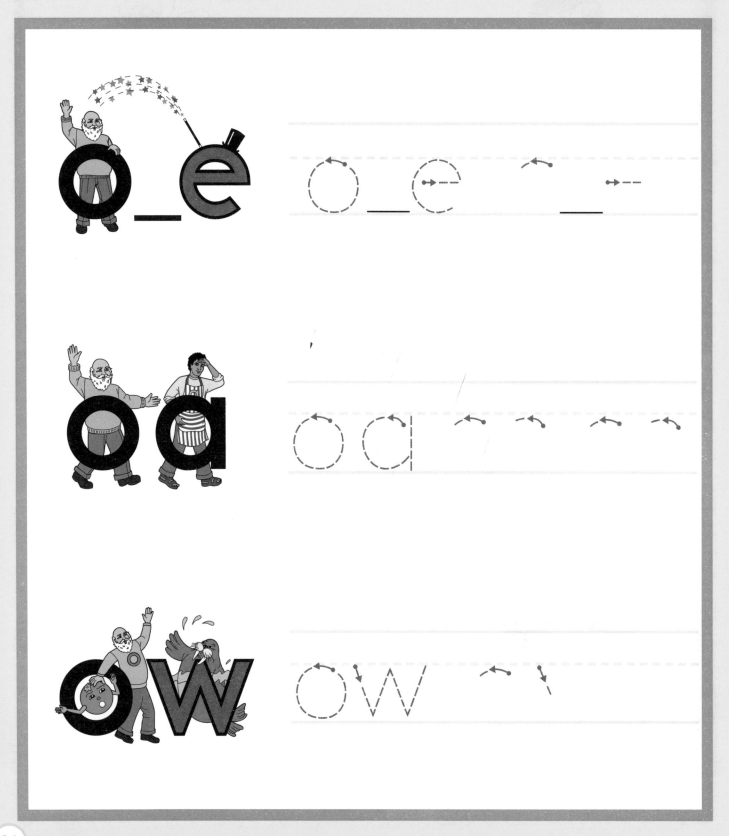

Write **o_e**, **oa** or **ow** on the lines to complete the words.

r _ p _

s _ _ p

g _ _ t

b _ _ t

sn _ _ _

ph _ n _

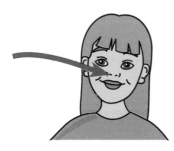

n _ s _

b _ _ l

c _ _ t

Let's write these letter shapes.

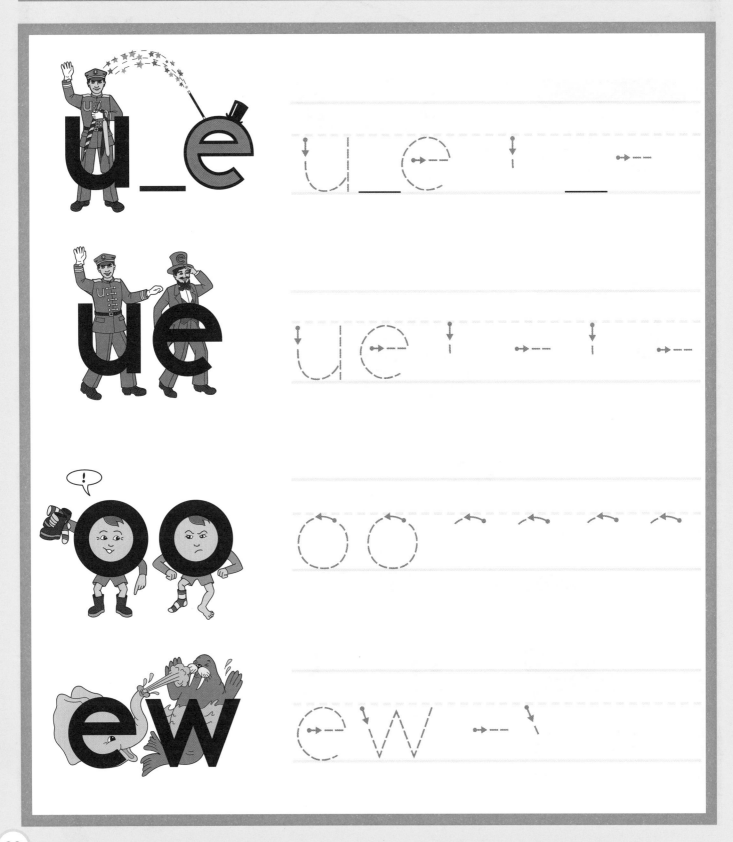

Write **u_e**, **ue**, **oo** or **ew** on the lines to complete the words.

bl____

n____s

T____sday
____

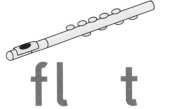

c_b_
__ __

f____d
__ __

fl_t_
__ __

gl____

sp____n

j____els

Let's write these letter shapes.

Look out when robots are about!

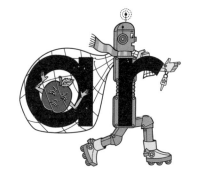

Write **ar** or **or** on the lines to complete the words.

c ___ ds

st ___ m

f __ k

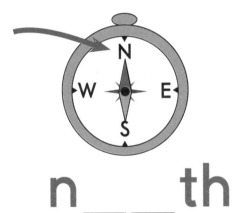

n ___ th

st ___

h ___ se

sc __ f

Let's write these letter shapes.

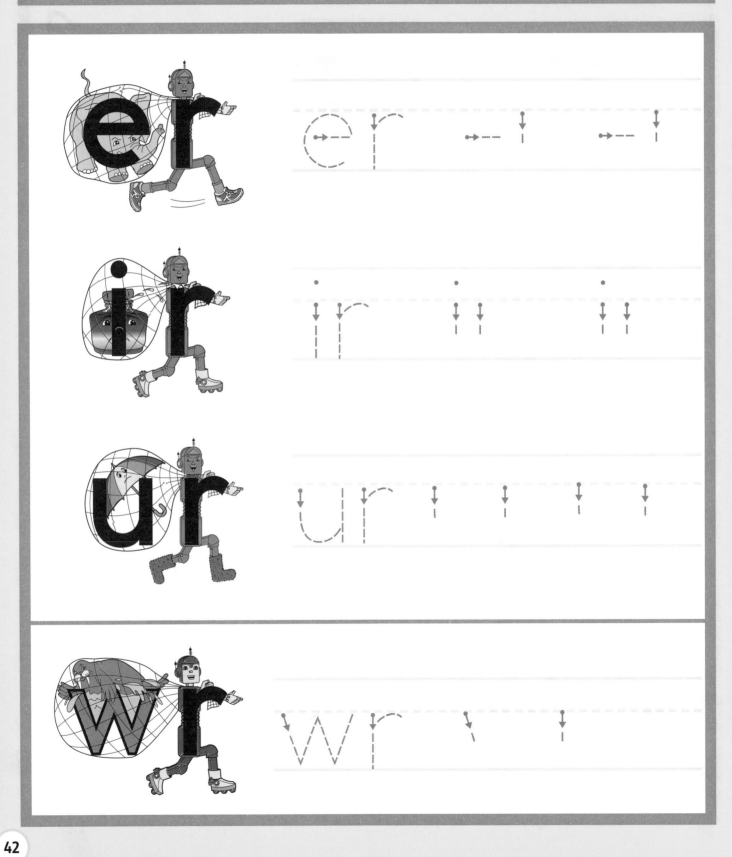

er

ir

ur

wr

Write **er**, **ir**, **ur** or **wr** on the lines to complete the words.

b___d

tig___

flow___s

ladd___

n___se

g___l

sk___t

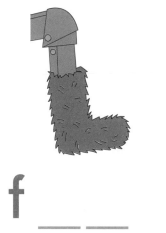

f___

___ite

Let's write these letter shapes.

Write **o**, **oo**, or **u** on the lines to complete the words.

b____k

p__sh

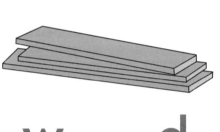

w____d

p__ll

d__ve

m____nkey

Let's write <u>these</u> <u>letter</u> shapes, and the words below.

Add 'oy' and read the sentence.

R__ is ann__ed that his

dog has destr__ed his

new t__.

46

Write **oy** or **oi** on the lines to complete the words.

b __ __ l

t __ __ s

b __ __ __

c __ __ ns

s __ __ l

t __ __ let

The _____

_____ the

rocket _____.

audience   applauded   launch

Write **aw** or **au** on the lines to complete the words.

___tumn

p___

y___n

l___nch

s___

astron___t

Let's write these letter shapes and the words below.

The cat had found a _____ coming ___ of the _____.

cow   ground   mouse   flower   out

Write **ow** or **ou** on the lines to complete the words.

f___ntain

t___n

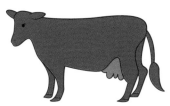

c____

v___els

m___se

m___tain

You can write lots of words now! Write the correct letters on the lines to make the words.

Fill in the missing words to complete the sentences.
The words you need are in the yellow space below.

A _____ on a _____.

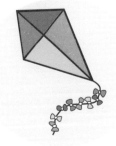

A _____ in the _____.

A _____ eats _____.

A _____ on a _____.

cake girl grapes car kite plate road sky

Draw lines from this robot capturing Mr A and Mr I to the things that include the robot puffing out hot **air**! Circle the one that doesn't.

Think of an **air** word and draw it.

Draw a line around the **air** words in the grid below. They go across and down.

c	h	a	i	r	w	s
f	a	j	o	e	h	t
a	i	c	a	o	l	a
i	r	v	g	r	e	i
r	n	m	f	a	i	r
y	p	a	i	r	b	s

stairs

fairy

hair

chair

fair

Can you find one more **air** word in the grid? Copy it on to the lines.

_____ _____ ____ ____

Look at the pictures and read the sentences below. Copy the correct sentence for each picture onto the dotted lines.

- I love reading stories about fairies.
- She likes going to the fair.
- She likes brushing her hair.

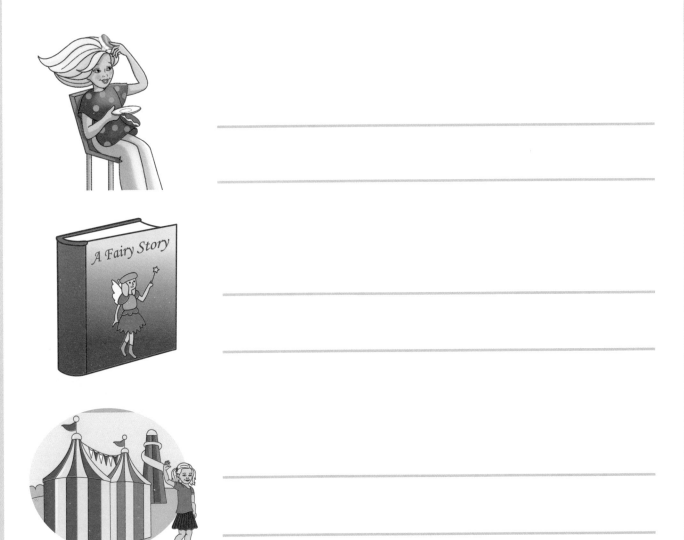

Fill in the missing words to complete the sentences.
The words you need are in the yellow space below.

I will dry my _____ ,

then go to the _____ .

The _____ is

on the _____ .

fair   fairy   hair   stairs

Draw lines from this robot capturing Mr E and Mr A to the things that include the robot puffing out hot air! Circle the one that doesn't.

Think of an **ear** word and draw it.

There are two sounds you might hear when you see these two Vowel Men behind a robot's back. Sometimes the robot puffs out hot air. But sometimes he points to his ear and says, "I can't hear!"

Look at the words below where the robot is saying, "I can't hear!"

ear

year

tears

hear

Draw lines to join each picture to its correct word and sound.

hear

year

pear

"I can't hear!"

Puffing out air.

59

Look at the pictures below. Tick a box for each difference in picture 2 and circle them on the picture.

Fill in the missing words to complete the sentences.
The words you need are in the yellow space below.

The _____ are

picking _____ .

I use my _____

to _____ .

bears   ears   hear   pears

A Day Trip to the Fair

The Letterlanders are at the fair! Search the picture for the things listed on the right. Then expand your vocabulary with new fairground words below.

Lucy's lollies

1st!

face painting

RING TOSS

PET SHOW

New vocabulary!

rosette

helter-skelter

candyfloss

Can you see:

a blue balloon
in the air?

Harry Hat Man on
the stairs?

a pair of coconuts?

an inflatable filled
with air?

something to help
people hear?

a parrot
quite near?

Write **air** or **ear** on the lines to complete these words, then match a sticker to each word.

air   ear

p _____ s

air   ear

st _____ s

air   ear

f _____ y

air   ear

b _____ s

Listen

Fill in the missing words to complete these sentences. Then listen and repeat the sentences.

Track 62

This pair are sitting on a _____.
Nick is pulling Golden Girl's ____.

This ____ has a balloon filled with ___.

Sentences

Read the sentence. Look at the 4 other words and see if you can substitute 1 or 2 words to make a new sentence.

I can hear a dog.	bear	fair	see	fairy

Example: I can see a fairy.

Read aloud

Check that the new sentence you have made make sense by reading them aloud to a partner.

Draw lines from Clever Cat as a hissing snake to the things that include her saying **ce**. Circle the one that doesn't.

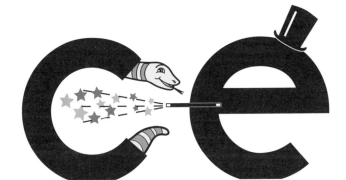

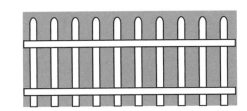

Think of a **ce** word and draw it.

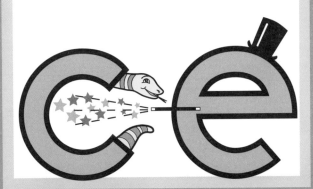

66

Read the sentences and complete the pictures with your stickers to match.

1. Stick a nice face on the boy.

2. Stick a fish on the rice.

3. Stick a rocket in space.

Write **ce** on the lines to complete these words.

ambulan_____

mi_____

i_____

fa_____

Can you think of any more **ce** words?

Draw lines from Clever Cat as a hissing snake to the **ci** words. Circle the one that isn't.

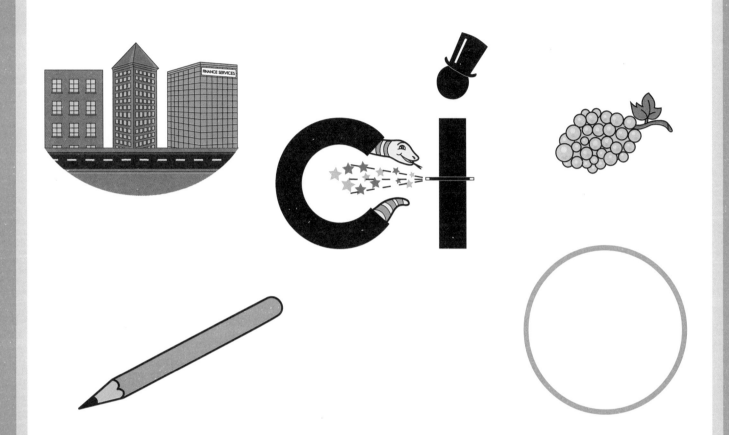

Draw something in this **ci**rcus tent!

Read the sentences and look at the pictures below. Copy the correct sentence for each picture onto the lines.

- Let's go to the city.
- Let's draw a circle.
- Let's all go to the circus.

Read the story. Write **ce** or **ci** on the lines to complete the words. Read the story again to a friend.

It is cold. There is i__ on the road.

The children like the __ty. There is

an excellent __nema. The children

skate to get to the __ty __nema.

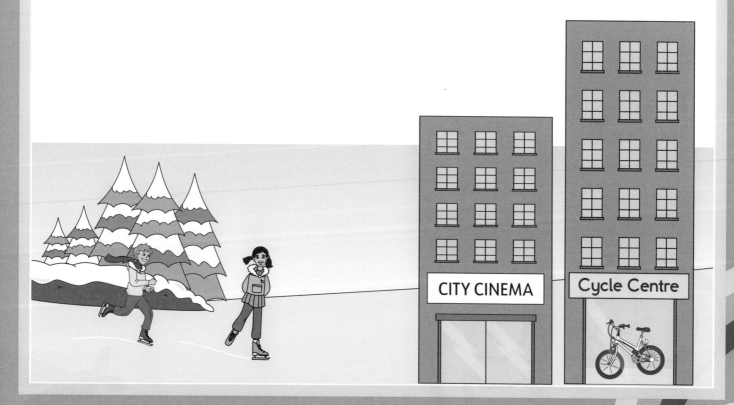

Draw lines from Clever Cat as a hissing snake to the **cy** words. Circle the thing that doesn't.

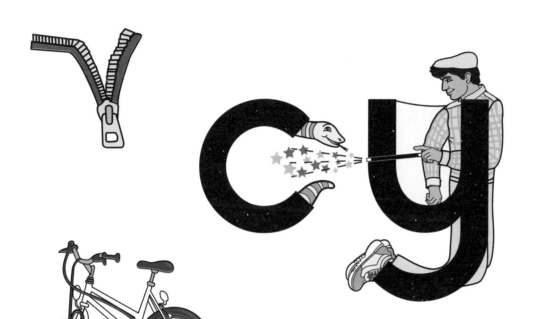

Can you draw some spi**cy** rice?

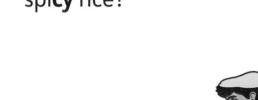

Fill in the missing words to complete the sentences.
The words you need are in the yellow space below.

Call a doctor. We need

an ambulance! It's

an _____ .

I like _____ in my

_____ after I _____ .

emergency   cycle   juice   ice

Grocery Shopping

The Letterlanders are grocery shopping! Search the picture for the things listed on the right. Then expand your vocabulary with the new words below.

New vocabulary!

citrus fruit

cereal

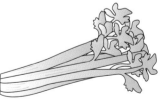

celery

Can you see:

some excellent cakes? ☐

a glass of grape juice? ☐

a packet of rice? ☐

a 1/2 price tag? ☐

the emergency exit? ☐

some nice lettuce? ☐

Use your stickers to label the picture below. Look in your books for help remembering the words.

Write down what the road is like.

It is _____ .

Draw a line around the **ce**, **ci** and **cy** words in the grid below. They go across and down.

f	x	y	g	i	c	e	c
a	r	z	b	b	p	l	i
c	y	l	i	n	d	e	r
e	d	r	c	c	n	s	c
c	i	k	y	s	w	p	l
i	s	p	c	w	e	a	e
t	g	j	l	s	h	c	x
y	u	i	e	e	v	e	s

face

space

city

bicycle

cylinder

circle

Can you think of one more word starting with **ci** to write on the lines?

_____ _____ _____ _____ _____ _____ _____

Listen

Listen to the words. Put a tick next to the correct spelling pattern. The first one has been done for you.

Track 69

How do you spell it?

1.

ce	ci	cy	s
✓	☐	☐	☐

2.

ce	ci	cy	s
☐	☐	☐	☐

3.

ce	ci	cy	s
☐	☐	☐	☐

4.

ce	ci	cy	s
☐	☐	☐	☐

5.

ce	ci	cy	s
☐	☐	☐	☐

Listen again

This exercise requires careful listening skills.
Listen more than once if you need to.